THE WEALTHY MINDSET

THE WEALTHY MINDSET

AURORA WINTERS

publisher logo
Revival Waves of Glory Books & Publishing

CONTENTS

CHAPTER 1

Introduction to the Wealthy Mindset

Research suggests that the main factor in determining personal success and happiness is the relationship an individual has with money and wealth. If someone has a negative relationship with money (believing it is the root of all evil or successive wealth is out of reach and only reserved for the fortunate), they are more likely to struggle with financial difficulties and live a less satisfying life. Although wealth is subjective and varies from person to person, it's important to note that material success is often considered a factor on the path to living a content and fulfilled life.

So what's the key to achieving this kind of happiness with money? It's transforming your mindset. A positive association with wealth can increase the likelihood of success, but society's negative attitudes can make people feel guilty, ashamed, or just plain uncomfortable about their financial success. The stereotype that wealthy people are somehow evil, dishonest, or just innately lucky can lead to both unkind judgments of the fortunate few and negative feelings about money itself. The problem is that these attitudes not only put a damper on wealth production, but they also affect one's confidence about aspirations in life.

Understanding the Importance of Mindset in Financial Success

Being wealthy is a mindset. What you think is what you manifest. With problems in how to relate to money - not enough of it, challenges in earning enough, or being too caught up with it - you are having problems in life. These problems, like all problems, tend to reflect deeper issues about your self-esteem. If self-esteem means honoring yourself, being true to yourself, how do you act? Do you know what is right for you and your situation? Because you are not clear about what you feel is right and need to break free from your negative programming, you question your feelings. When it comes to money matters, you may doubt your own judgment. You may have money, but it does not come easily. You work for every penny, and most of your energy is spent in worry about not having enough. It is not the kind of life you want, but you do not know how to get out of the mess you are in.

When you think about wealth, what words or images come up for you? Money, mansions, fourth and fifth homes, extravagant cars, vacations, freedom? Are these signs of wealth or the cause of wealth? At the College of Metaphysics, students refer to their pursuit as acquiring financial freedom or whatever is necessary to be free to build and express their dreams. Freedom has a much broader range of possibilities than just money. Look at the lives of historical people such as Jesus, Mother Theresa, or Gandhi. They were not wealthy by the traditional meaning of the word, but they were doing what they loved, what they were built to do. They were free to use all of their potential for serving the world. As Erich Fromm pointed out, they had the courage to be in a world that often does not think with its own mind or feel with its own soul.

CHAPTER 2

Identifying and Overcoming Limiting Beliefs

To question our money beliefs, we have to first understand our financial values. What do you innately consider is right and wrong with respect to money? Once you've made a list of what you value with money, you can check that list to see if what you believe in is manifesting as self-satisfying, self-defeating, or serving some other end. You should start identifying and attacking each limiting belief one at a time, listing as many positive facts as possible. You might be pleasantly surprised to find that cutting the legs from under these deeply ingrained beliefs will yield significant emotional freedom and release as you clear the clutter from your relationship with money.

The first step necessary to break free of damaging financial scripts is to figure out exactly what you believe in the first place. For some of us, much of what we think about money comes from the behaviors of our parents, friends, or relatives. Actively questioning our assumptions and examining where they originated is a crucial step in reforming our thought patterns and perceptions. From that position of awareness and understanding, we can then make our decisions not simply on autopilot, but as true acts of free will.

Common Money Myths and Misconceptions

Perhaps without realizing, we have been schooled in a few notions about money and what it truly means. Everyone has heard the advice, "Money doesn't grow on trees." The implication is that money is finite, but money is not a physical thing and so it's not finite as in having a limited amount. The availability of money is not a matter of scarcity but instead is determined by thoughts about money. If it's true that our beliefs do indeed create our reality (and it's very much a fact), why should money be viewed differently? Why should it be considered different from any other thing in our reality? But it is treated differently, and often considered prime among our problems and concerns. Would it surprise you to learn that more people worry about money problems than health concerns? In order to gain a new appreciation for the true importance of money, we first need to become aware of the common everyday myths and misconceptions about money.

Valerie Gilbert is the author of four books on the subject of Applied Metaphysics. She left her three-decades-old career as a writer for Broadway in order to write about how to apply the esoteric great metaphysical and magical laws of life to everyday life. Ms. Gilbert reconciles spirituality with practicality and presents the subject of manifesting wealth as a highly desirable lifestyle rather than a religious concept.

THE BOOK PROVIDES: - How to purge your negative beliefs about money and replace them with empowering thoughts - The spiritual importance of "giving back" - The four wealth-building factors - The role of thoughts in creating money or debt - The question of self-worth - Your spiritual wealth in terms of your bank balance and the real value of your home - The meaning of empty pockets but a heart full of dreams - The essential principle of prosperity - that provision follows vision

"The Wealthy Mindset: Transforming Your Relationship with Money" by Valerie Gilbert provides the practical techniques and mindset adjustments that will teach you how to live a truly wealthy life. If it's an actual wealth that you're seeking, then mastering your internal dialogues and reassessing your beliefs with regard to money will be essential. The author shows from her own experience how completely liberating it is to re-evaluate what truly matters most. "The Wealthy Mindset" offers a refreshing, enlightening perspective of money. As the author points out, money has only the power that we each consciously and collectively give to it. Surrender your negative attitudes and money anxiety to a higher power, and you will no longer be a slave to money. Join millions of others who have unplugged from the work-eat-pay-die grind. It must be comforting to know that the key to wealth is within. "The Wealthy Mindset" will give you the blueprint you need to unlock the door to financial independence and freedom.

CHAPTER 3

Cultivating a Positive Relationship with Money

Discover the source. When it comes to cultivating a positive relationship with money, the raw and unadulterated truth is that creating a maximum amount of wealth and abundance can be achieved only when you are at peace with your soul and with this particular concept. To create and sustain an abundant lifestyle successfully, you must desire wealth on a deep and emotional level, where it becomes a spiritual quest of the heart, a cosmic desire to be rewarded for all that you do and desire to be recompensed for the love, compassion, and service that you personally provide.

Successfully achieving an abundant mindset requires cultivating a positive relationship with money. Many of us grew up with certain attitudes around money, some inherited from our parents, the media, or the greater socioeconomic atmosphere, otherwise known as the collective consciousness. However, with some effort and a little bit of retraining, it is completely possible to change this long-standing relationship with money into an association characterized by love, joy, gratitude, and positivity. Here are several concrete steps to help propel you onto the path of love and prosperity.

Practical Strategies for Shifting Your Money Mindset

Do your homework. Invest time to explore whether it is worth spending more money just because it is more expensive. It is uninformed that purchases are based on price. Personal finance and consumer advocates will tell you that often the most important thing is usually the budget image. Before parting with your hard-earned money, investigate all categories of real estate and sales taxes.

Round up your purchases. When shopping, round up your total purchase, even if it is just a few coins.

Calculate your current spending. The first step to changing your financial situation is to be fully aware of your current spending patterns. Spend 30 days noting every expenditure. Calculate it and study it carefully. Sum it up in categories. As you turn to your new financial life, it will be necessary to differentiate between your necessary and discretionary spending. Once that's done, identify specific ways you can cut your spending. Once you've decided what to cut, consider using your savings for products. Whenever you earn a living, your earnings are more important than the cost of your earnings. Simply stated, keep your costs down and don't buy anything extra. As you move towards a better place in your whole life, it's okay to prevent your children from checking their ideas or wishes.

Changing your money mindset is not just a matter of recognizing your self-defeating beliefs and replacing them with positive ones. It's a process of consistent action that results from a complete transformation of your relationship with money. The following are practical strategies that will help you make that transformation.

CHAPTER 4

The Power of Goal Setting and Visualization

How does mental visualization work? In many ways, mental visualization works due to the Reticular Activating System (RAS) in our brain. The RAS is the part of the brain known for its ability to bring relevant information to the conscious mind and for distinguishing between levels of importance of information that enters through our five senses. Whenever we neurologically hardwire our brains for success or failure by thinking and visualizing both in negative and positive terms, it becomes pretty easy to predict the outcome. The person who uses mental visualization techniques to succeed in life is doing so through their body's conscious and subconscious preparation for success. Most people who are successful mentally practice this mind-over-matter power without even realizing it. That's because in sports, business, and every endeavor, those with a Mind Game have a Leg Up.

It is a concept in the books "Think and Grow Rich" and "The Power of Positive Thinking" that aligns with modern scientific discoveries concerning the power of the mind and the effect the mind has upon the body. The concept states that anything you envision and believe in your mind's eye, you can achieve. There are countless stories of individuals using mental visualization to help them achieve what at first seemed like an impossible goal. But reality is, envisioning and believing aren't enough. You can't sit down, clear your mind, focus on a desired objective, and expect a fat check to arrive in the mail if what you are doing isn't in alignment with the mental picture you are painting. The concept isn't a form of magic but rather a powerful state of mind that has physical and psychological effects upon the body.

Setting SMART Financial Goals

The greatest wealth created in the third world has come about during the last twenty years in countries that adopt democracy and free-market capitalism. It's not just the wealthy that should have written financial goals. Everyone should take the time to sit down, set their financial goals, and make sure that they have SMART financial objectives that let them know that they are on the road to achieving them.

Time-Bound: Your short-term financial goals help keep you on course for your intermediary financial goals, which in turn ensure that you do not lose sight of your long-term financial goals. Have a time limit and work hard to meet the deadline. How long do you have before retirement? What must be achieved within a certain period of time in order to meet deadlines?

Relevant: The only goal that is truly yours is the one that you have chosen to achieve despite official or societal obligations. Your life plan is unique, and your financial goals and plan should reflect this. Are you saving enough to provide for the lifestyle you want in retirement?

Attainable: If your life's goal is to amass a billion dollars, and you barely graduated from high school, odds are you will not succeed. Be realistic and honest with yourself. Can you invest enough to achieve your financial goals? Make sure that your plan is something you can afford.

Measurable: This could mean that you need to work with your advisor to quantify things that are not exact so that you can track your progress along the way to financial peace of mind. How much money do you need to save? What is the interest rate you need to achieve on your investments? How much will you receive from your company pension? Your business has sales goals. They know how many customers they need and make sure they achieve the necessary number of sales monthly to reach target. Your business also has expense goals, and they ensure that monthly expenses do not exceed revenue.

Specific: Do not set general goals (e.g., "I want to be rich"). Have an exact idea of your objective ("I want a million dollars"). How much money do you need to guarantee financial peace of mind? Make sure that you and your partner have a shared objective. It is okay that a woman wants to work for a few more years and that a man wants to retire yesterday. However, mutual agreement on when and where is important.

When Henry Ford invented the motorcar in 1903, he had two objectives: to make cars affordable and to pay his workers twice the industry standard. The goal of paying his workers above the market rate generated further wealth through the workforce spending their extra money on the products his company made. In life and business you need to set financial goals that are SMART:

Successful people set goals. They set goals and then work out how to achieve them. Unsuccessful people do not set goals. Rather, they go with the flow. Their careers and lives tend to be haphazard and unstructured. Very often, they end up getting nowhere and blaming the world for their circumstances. What is true for an individual is true for a partnership or a family. In the absence of clearly defined financial goals and objectives, partners and families can end up going nowhere and blaming others for their lack of financial success.

Setting Financial Goals - SMART Financial Goals Ideally, you and your partner should discuss your own respective definitions of wealth and be sure that they are complementary; doing so provides you with shared long-term financial goals for your relationship. Most people are under the misimpression that wealth creation can only occur later in life; the truth is that you can and should start a sound program of financial goal setting and wealth creation as soon as possible. It is important to have short-term, intermediate, and long-term financial goals. Remember that if you do not know where you are going, you'll probably end up someplace else.

CHAPTER 5

Building Wealth Through Investments

The such basics that everyone should seek to understand. What if you were earning 90% per year on your money? How long would it take you to become a millionaire? Ten years! If somebody is earning more than 10% on their money, they're certainly not paying cash for your car. Why should they start? Even during depressions, it is not uncommon for people to earn between 20-30% on their money. Why shouldn't they use this advantage to work towards financial independence? If you learn to appreciate this power, by seeking to understand it, you will have taken a big step towards the right investment mentality.

My grandfather used to say, "If you have ten dollars in your pocket, five are spent." At the time, this piece of advice was astounding wisdom. It spoke to the reality that we cannot grow money without first knowing how to manage it. Here, we will assume that you are an expert at making money, and you wish to manage it effectively. We will talk about building wealth by acquiring assets. It hasn't been until recent history that this has become possible for the average man. Before, only the very rich had access to these tools, but because of modern financial planning, anyone with the proper mindset can have an asset portfolio that rivals the tycoons of years past.

Types of Investments and Their Risk-Return Profiles

I used an old, rather than popular, definition of investments at the start of this chapter because I want to first be clear about what I mean here when I refer to investments before I also discuss how to make your money and income produce the lifestyle you want. In as broad and inclusive terms as possible, an investment is any expenditure in the present that, if incurred and sustained wisely, is expected, with a minimum of risk, to increase a person's annual income or produce other benefits over time. Properly applied, this definition covers all the ways in which a person or family can spend money and time to preserve and protect a family's economic future. It necessitates ensuring that you have carefully explored all the possible uses to which you could put your money and labor, where doing so would seem likely to increase the overall spending power or quality of life of your family in the long run.

CHAPTER 6

Practicing Financial Discipline and Responsibility

The essence of being financially comfortable is very simple. It involves knowing your financial status, employing long-term financial planning, creating personal fortification, embracing your earnings and spending, encouraging beneficial financial habits, maintaining discipline, and utilizing self-restraint. Even though they may say, "Why do tomorrow what I can spend today?" they act differently. They also know that practicing financial discipline is actually doing themselves a favor today, because their future will be richer and more enjoyable.

Simply, being wealthy means having more money than you require to live comfortably, while being financially comfortable means having enough to make you feel secure. The wealthy, however, have freely welcomed money into their lives so they can live life more fully. They also seek to increase their personal wealth as a way of ensuring that they will not be a burden on society should they need assistance in the future. This ambitious, responsible approach to money is part of their need to belong to society, and to be independent and valuable individuals. The key difference between a wealthy person and a financially comfortable person is in their attitudes toward money, and how they manage it. This difference allows the wealthy to increase their wealth and live wealthier lives.

Budgeting and Tracking Expenses

The more you can track down all your spending in the present, the less money has of slipping out of your retirement fund in the way-past future. This is true for excessive spending as well as for too little spending. Be sure to include unexpected taxes as well as the more expected holidays and gifts in your annual expenses. If you do not get a yearly bonus, do not spend as if you do. If some people just cannot seem to find enough money and others must give it away, whether you call them wealthy or poor is a questionable choice. To many people, if you have so much money that you do not have to work, if you actually have enough to take four long holidays a year and remodel both your house and your face whenever the spirit moves you, then I am afraid that you simply must be wealthy.

For many people, and possibly even more so in couples, the word budgeting is right up there with some of the more unmentionable four-letter ones. It is important to realize that a budget or spending plan does not necessarily mean abject self-denial, whereas a whizz at budgeting is not necessarily a wealthy mover and shaker. The key is using a budget to discern how a finite income can cover an infinite extravaganza. The budget is a means of knowing how to do it, not a means to line up each indulgence and put it before the chopping block. To replace mindless extravagance with confident, lavish living is not a paradox. It is the essence of a wealthy mindset. Spend, then save.

CHAPTER 7

Overcoming Financial Setbacks and Bouncing Back St

Practicing crisis management with finances is extremely critical if you are to achieve great wealth in your lifetime. Overcoming financial setbacks and bouncing back stronger is a key component to nurturing a positive relationship with money. When you suffer from a financial setback, what is your normal reaction? Are you the kind of person who realizes that money loss is just temporary and takes steps to plan a financial recovery, or does the setback seem to create a bottomless pit that so often appears too hard to climb out of?

Give financial advice and consulting to others, but ensure also that you refrain from making the same financial mistakes that millions of other people are prone to make by following the advice you offer others. That way, others will also take your advice more seriously.

There are many types of financial setbacks that can happen, especially when you are striving to achieve wealth. Whether it is borrowing money to start your own business or investing a good part of your savings into a particular investment, only for that asset to tumble. These situations that you may find yourself in will not only test your character but can also put a great strain on your finances. So it is important to react in the right way to ensure that the effects are minimized and the healing process can begin.

Resilience and Adaptability in Financial Planning
Achieving a high level of financial resilience or adaptability is a developmental process that allows a person to thrive during or following any of the many potentially significant life changes, including underemployment or joblessness, disability or illness, family growth or shrinkage through marriage or divorce, birth of a child or death of a spouse or other family member, as well as many other significant changes that can affect our lives such as natural disasters, crime victimization, emergencies, and many other potentially traumatic events. But it can be very fulfilling to break free of one's financial comfort zone, tap previously unknown resources and talents, and stride boldly toward achieving results, to demonstrate that an overhaul of some retirement planning, college financing, or estate planning concepts without prior warning is merely a distraction. After all, the vast majority of the truly important lifetime financial goals usually take decades or even longer to produce laudable achievements or end results."

"In the face of the rapidly changing, complex, high-stakes world in which we live, it's extremely important for people to develop the skills to achieve resilience and adaptability in their own financial planning process. Events or situations can result in profound changes overnight, making it necessary for individuals to go back to "the drawing board" to identify their financial management priorities and possibly to develop entirely new strategies to guide their efforts and make progress. People who haven't yet learned to be adaptable and flexible can become overwhelmed in response to a sudden change in their environment, leading to an unproductive, even paralyzed, financial sense of panic.

CHAPTER 8

The Role of Generosity and Giving Back in Wealth B

Compassion is a vital aspect to wealth and one way to make money. For most, the correlation between compassion and money is seen as a one-way coin, with money serving only as a generator facilitating dispensation. Certain individuals just insist on doing the proof, consistently showing that giver and receiver alike are both enriched and beautified. A good measure of caution is always governed by common sense. Rich or poor, most of us cannot afford to take advantage of or be taken advantage of by others. Developing a wealth mindset involves taking the long view and scouting possible pitfalls through experience and clear thinking. Murky thoughts and shallow convictions can inadvertently scorch and tarnish the most generous of intentions. While sympathy for the misfortune is required, respect for their prowess and self-worth should be equally communicated to smooth the interaction. Mindset is the creator of wealth and money, just like love and trust, open the doors to a brand new world.

Understanding one's worth is also about understanding one's spiritual heritage. Adopting a wealthy mindset and having money reflect those energies, however, is only part of the equation. Without fail, wealthy individuals believe that true wealth begins only when they start helping others realize their dreams. Part of this generosity comes from the attunement of that delight they enjoy. They know others deserve similar comfort and delight in expressing and acquiring what they need. In a growing world of hope, there are plenty of unmet needs where a generous nature can bestow great benefits and satisfy immense cravings. With part of that transmitted delight enriching the lives of others, these generous individuals are not only keenly aware, they know that hope is constantly flowing back into their lives, leaving satisfaction as the byproduct.

Impactful Ways to Contribute to Causes You Care About

At its core, the Comfort Zone wealthy mindset is all about cultivating unwavering belief in ourselves, our own talents, and value. It is about embracing ambition and drive in reaching our personal goals and financial success. Fundamentally, this is what developing a wealthy mindset is all about. It's about knowing that we can achieve these goals if we work hard and continue to grow. The Comfort Zone focuses on comfort and enjoyment; affluence and opulence do not interest us. We want to be worry-free and appreciate peace of mind. We place significance on our game of the Material World at this level and place importance on living a meaningful life. It's about transforming our relationship with money, and it would be fair to say that those with a wealthy mindset are in flow where money is concerned, unlike the scarcity mindset where the cycle of debt is ever present.

When it comes to money, each person has their own unique energetic patterns and beliefs where it is concerned. This includes both the need for money and one's own worthiness to receive and keep it. Interestingly, many people who have money struggles are often those with a desire to make a big difference in this world. After our personal and spiritual growth, many of us come to a point where life changes from being all about us to wanting to contribute to things and people we believe in. So it stands to reason that we also begin to contribute and participate in charitable actions and those who are less fortunate than ourselves. This is very often a way of actually gifting to ourselves. However, once we have realized personal success, money becomes of lesser concern to us, as developing a wealthy mindset is all about creating a life without financial struggle. Instead, we have moved from a position of survival to that of wanting to thrive. Our Comfort Zone values now become focused on creating a meaningful life, and we place more importance on contributing to our purpose.

CHAPTER 9

Maintaining a Wealthy Mindset for Long-Term Succes

The key to financial success is to maintain a long-term wealthy mindset, and your wealth will be sustained. No matter what your goals are, you must always treat yourself with respect and dignity. Of course, any good strategy includes some backup plans. Throughout life, even the most prudent planners have temporary slumps where money is tight or is not coming in quickly enough. By making your income hinge on your skills and expertise or unrivaled top-notch products and services, you will rise again to soar to new heights as a comfortable, effective sensation. In every field and in every line of work, some people outshine the others. You can be that person.

Even with all the great strategies and methods I share with you in this book, it is possible for you to have a temporary period of wealth or financial success followed by financial ruin. Look around you and on the internet, and you'll hear countless stories of lottery winners who end up throwing away millions as they burn bridges with family and friends or simply squander the savings on poor investment choices and careless spending. People who come into money, when they haven't developed the character to support the wealth, seldom hold onto it for long.

Strategies for Consistently Nurturing a Positive Money Mindset

Making (or Remaking) Commitments to Financial Wealth and Splendor If you are truly desirous of and serious in your commitment to use a wealthy mindset to help your financial desires unfold, record your answers to the questions below. Be explicit about your pledge, purpose, consequences, and specific areas you desire to impact or focus on, including how you would like your actions or self to grow or evolve uniquely in each area. Response data collection use only; DO NOT DISTRIBUTE.

What will it take for you to maintain a positive and expectant money mindset from this day forward? This chapter discusses strategies for: • Shoring up your "fruition faith" - believing that your ideas and efforts can bring financial abundance and other desires to fruition - so it can't waver in the face of skepticism. • Incorporating daily, weekly, monthly, and quarterly routines to consistently center your thinking mind on deeper trust, greater possibility, and persistence in translating your ideas into cash flow. These suggestions help to orbit your spending of money and time strategically around environments and energies that naturally support your financial abundance.